The AI Revolution: Strategies For Business Growth Amid Disruption

Robert Culpepper

StoryUp Media

TABLE OF CONTENTS

INTRODUCTION:

It may seem unusual, or even odd, to see a print book about Artificial Intelligence (AI) in a world where technology evolves at breakneck speed. By the time the ink on this book dries, another groundbreaking advancement in AI may very well have reshaped the landscape once again. However, I have written this book as a snapshot of where things stand today, January 2025 *(Last-minute update, 21 Jan, President Trump announces $500 billion AI infrastructure investment in the US).*

As this book is about AI, you might be wondering: "Did I write this book, or was it written by AI?" And that would be a fair question. The truth is that it was a collaborative effort. I created the outline, crafted the title, and wrote the description, along with the front and back matter. The content was generated with the assistance of AI. Yet, this process was not without its challenges; I invested additional time in editing to ensure the text was human reader friendly. After all, AI often creates content that strays into the realm of hallucinations and absurdities!

So, what AI tool did I use? I utilized my own book-writing tool, *"InstantAuthorAI.com,"* By the time you delve into these pages, I may have started other projects or taken on new clients. It has been an excellent AI writing assistant, but I tend to create projects, finish them, then my curiosity leads me elsewhere, like clients. I prefer working with clients! The human-to-human connection is something AI will never be able to replace (at least today!) and to which I am forever grateful!

And finally, a BIG shoutout to Liz at LizPepper.com, who's also a registered designer at Canva, designed my cool cover, did the book layout and formatting while remaining calm and supportive through my many last-minute changes!

OK, there you go. I hope you find value in, *"The AI Revolution: Strategies for Business Growth Amid Disruption."* Should you wish to learn more about my work as a sales, marketing and AI consultant (fractional CMO, CGO... CAIO) I invite you to visit my website, RobertCulpepper.me. You can also email me at AIRbook@RobertCulpepper.me. I read every email and do my best to respond to each one!

Thank you for joining me on this journey through the "AI Revolution".

Robert Culpepper
Barcelona, Spain
Jan 2025

CHAPTER 1: UNDERSTANDING AI AND ITS IMPACT

"By far, the greatest danger of Artificial Intelligence is that people conclude too early that they understand it."

Eliezer Yudkowsky

American computer scientist and researcher

What is Artificial Intelligence (AI)?

Artificial Intelligence (AI) refers to the simulation of human intelligence in machines programmed to think and learn like humans. This technology encompasses various subfields, including machine learning, Natural Language

Processing (NLP), robotics, and computer vision. In essence, AI enables machines to carry out tasks that typically require human intelligence, such as understanding language, recognizing patterns, making decisions, and solving problems. For businesses of all sizes, understanding AI is crucial as it offers opportunities to enhance efficiency, improve customer experiences, and foster innovation.

One of the most significant aspects of AI is its ability to analyze vast amounts of data quickly and accurately. Businesses generate an enormous amount of data every day, and AI can help extract valuable insights from this information. By leveraging AI-powered analytics, business owners can identify trends, understand customer behavior, and make data-driven decisions. This capability can lead to improved marketing strategies, optimized operations, and ultimately, increased profitability. For small and medium enterprises (SMEs), adopting AI technologies can level the playing field, allowing them to compete more effectively with larger corporations. AI also plays a crucial role in automating routine tasks, freeing up valuable time and resources for business owners and their employees. Automation can streamline processes such as customer support, inventory management, and financial reporting. By implementing AI-driven tools like chatbots or automated invoicing systems, businesses can enhance operational efficiency and reduce human error. This shift not only improves productivity but also enables staff to focus on more strategic initiatives, fostering innovation and growth within the organization.

Moreover, AI's impact on customer engagement cannot be overstated. Personalized experiences have become essential in today's competitive landscape, and AI excels at delivering tailored interactions. Through machine learning algorithms, businesses can analyze customer data to provide personalized recommendations, targeted marketing campaigns, and improved service offerings. For SMEs, leveraging AI to enhance customer relationships can result in increased loyalty and higher retention rates, ultimately driving long-term success.

However, as AI continues to evolve, it raises questions about its implications for the future of businesses. While it presents numerous opportunities, there are also concerns regarding job displacement, privacy, and ethical considerations. Business owners must navigate these challenges carefully, ensuring they adopt AI responsibly and transparently. By understanding what AI is and how it can benefit their operations, SMEs can harness its potential while addressing the associated risks, positioning themselves for success in an increasingly AI-driven world.

Historical Overview of AI Development

The history of Artificial Intelligence (AI) is a narrative that spans several decades, reflecting the evolution of technology and human understanding of intelligence itself. The roots of AI can be traced back to the mid-20th century, when pioneers like Alan Turing proposed theories about machine intelligence and computation. Turing's work laid the groundwork for the notion that machines could potentially simulate human thought processes. This period also saw the development of the first neural networks, which aimed to mimic the human brain's functioning. However, progress was slow, and interest dropped driven by reduced funding and skepticism regarding the feasibility of AI.

In the 1980s and 1990s, interest in AI began to resurge, driven by advances in computer power and the emergence of new techniques such as expert systems. These systems utilized rule-based logic to solve specific problems, providing businesses with tools to automate decision-making processes. While these early applications showcased AI's potential, they were often limited in scope, requiring extensive human intervention and expertise to maintain. Nevertheless, businesses started to

7

explore these technologies, recognizing their ability to enhance operational efficiency and customer engagement.

The turn of the millennium marked a significant shift in AI development, as the convergence of big data, improved algorithms, and increased computational power propelled the field forward. Machine learning, particularly deep learning, emerged as a dominant force, enabling systems to learn from vast amounts of data without explicit programming. This advancement allowed AI to tackle more complex tasks, from image and speech recognition to predictive analytics. For businesses, this meant access to tools that could analyze market trends, optimize supply chains, and personalize customer experiences in ways that were previously unimaginable.

In recent years, the integration of AI into everyday business practices has accelerated. Technologies such as chatbots, recommendation engines, and automated customer service solutions have become commonplace. SMEs are increasingly adopting these tools to remain competitive, streamline operations, and enhance customer satisfaction. As businesses harness the power of AI, the question of whether it will be a friend or a foe becomes crucial. The potential for increased efficiency and innovation is tempered by concerns about job displacement, ethical considerations, and reliance on technology that may not always align with human values.

Looking ahead, the future of AI development will likely bring both challenges and opportunities for SMEs. The ongoing evolution of AI technologies will necessitate a strategic approach to adoption, balancing the benefits of automation with the need for a human touch in customer interactions. Additionally, businesses will need to navigate the ethical landscape of AI, ensuring that their implementations foster trust and transparency. As AI continues to advance, understanding its historical context will be essential for business leaders to make informed decisions that align with their goals and values in an increasingly automated world.

The Current State of AI Technology

The current state of AI technology offers a landscape that is both promising and complex, particularly for SMEs. As the capabilities of AI continues to evolve, businesses are finding a myriad of applications that can enhance operational efficiency, improve customer engagement, and drive innovation. From chatbots that streamline customer service to predictive analytics that inform business strategies, the integration of AI into everyday operations is becoming increasingly essential for maintaining competitive advantage.

One of the most significant developments in AI technology is the rise of machine learning and deep learning algorithms. These technologies are enabling businesses to process vast amounts of data in real-time, uncovering insights that were previously unattainable. For SMEs, this means they can leverage data to make informed decisions, optimize supply chains, and personalize marketing efforts. The ability to harness data effectively can level the playing field, allowing smaller businesses to compete with larger corporations that traditionally have had more resources at their disposal.

Natural Language Processing (NLP) is another area where AI is making strides. Business owners can implement NLP tools to enhance communications, both internally and with customers. For instance, AI-driven virtual assistants can manage scheduling, respond to inquiries, and even generate reports. This not only frees up human resources for more strategic tasks but also improves response times and customer satisfaction. The increasing sophistication of NLP technology allows even small businesses to adopt solutions that enhance their operational capabilities without requiring extensive technical knowledge.

Despite the advantages, some business owners remain cautious about adopting AI technology. Concerns about data privacy, security, and the potential for job displacement are prevalent. It is crucial for SMEs to navigate these challenges thoughtfully. By investing in robust security measures and developing clear policies around data usage, businesses can mitigate risks associated with AI implementation. Furthermore, upskilling employees to work alongside AI tools can alleviate fears of job loss and help create a culture of collaboration between humans and machines.

The future trajectory of AI will likely dictate the success of businesses across various sectors. For SMEs, the choice to embrace AI can be a differentiating factor that propels growth and innovation. As technology continues to advance, staying informed about trends and developments in AI will be vital. Business owners must not only recognize AI as a tool for efficiency but also as a strategic partner that can drive their businesses forward in an increasingly competitive landscape.

CHAPTER 2: THE BENEFITS OF AI FOR SMALL AND MEDIUM ENTERPRISES (SMES)

"Before we work on artificial intelligence why don't we
do something about natural stupidity?"

Steve Polyak

Stephen Polyak, Ph.D. Artificial Intelligence

Enhancing Efficiency and Productivity

The integration of AI into business operations has proven to be a game-changer for SMEs. By automating routine tasks, AI allows business owners to redirect their focus toward strategic planning and customer engagement.

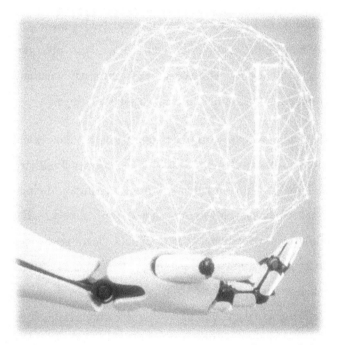

Tools such as chatbots, automated scheduling, and data analysis software can handle repetitive tasks more efficiently than human counterparts. This not only reduces operational costs but also ensures that resources are allocated to areas that drive growth and innovation.

AI-driven analytics can significantly enhance productivity by providing valuable insights into customer behavior and market trends. For SMEs, understanding their target audience is crucial for crafting effective marketing strategies. AI tools can process massive amounts of data, revealing patterns and preferences that would be difficult for humans to identify. By leveraging these insights, businesses can tailor their offerings, optimize pricing strategies, and improve customer satisfaction, resulting in increased sales and loyalty.

Moreover, AI can streamline supply chain management, which is often a challenge for small businesses. Predictive analytics can forecast demand more accurately, helping firms manage inventory levels effectively. This minimizes overstock and stockouts, leading to cost savings and improved cash flow. Additionally, AI can enhance supplier relationship management by analyzing performance data and providing recommendations for better collaboration. This holistic approach to supply chain efficiency not only improves productivity but also strengthens the overall business model.

Implementing AI solutions also fosters a culture of innovation within SMEs. As employees become accustomed to utilizing AI tools, they can explore new ways to enhance their workflows and deliver value to customers. This shift encourages a collaborative environment where team members feel empowered to experiment and share ideas. Businesses that embrace this mindset are more likely to adapt to emerging trends and technologies, ensuring they stay competitive in an ever-evolving market landscape.

However, the successful integration of AI requires a thoughtful approach. Business owners must evaluate their specific needs and choose the right tools that align with their goals. Training staff to effectively use AI is equally important, as employee buy-in is crucial for maximizing the benefits of these tools. By prioritizing efficiency and productivity through strategic AI integration, SMEs can position themselves for long-term success, transforming potential challenges into opportunities for growth.

Improving Customer Experience

Improving customer experience has become a critical focus for SMEs, especially in an era increasingly dominated by AI. As customers demand more personalized interactions and faster service, businesses must leverage AI to meet these expectations. AI

15

technologies can analyze customer data, identify patterns, and provide insights that help businesses understand their clientele better. By utilizing these insights, businesses can tailor their offerings, improving satisfaction and loyalty.

One of the most effective applications of AI in enhancing customer experience is through chatbots and virtual assistants. These tools can provide immediate responses to customer inquiries, ensuring that businesses remain accessible around the clock. For SMEs, which may not have the resources to maintain large customer service teams, AI-powered chatbots can handle a variety of tasks from answering Frequently Asked Questions (FAQs) to assisting with order placements. This not only improves response times but also frees up human staff to focus on more complex issues that require personal attention.

Another valuable application of AI is predictive analytics, which enables businesses to anticipate customer needs and preferences. By analyzing past purchasing behavior and trends, AI systems can suggest products or services that customers are likely to be interested in. This proactive approach not only enhances the shopping experience but also drives sales as customers are presented with tailored recommendations that resonate with their preferences.

SMEs that adopt predictive analytics can create a more engaging shopping experience, which in turn fosters customer loyalty and repeat business.

Personalization does not stop at product recommendations; it extends to marketing efforts as well. AI can help businesses segment their customer bases more effectively, allowing for targeted marketing campaigns that speak directly to specific groups. By analyzing demographic data, purchase history, and online behavior, businesses can craft messages that resonate with individual customers. This level of personalization can significantly increase engagement rates and conversion, making marketing efforts more efficient and effective.

Finally, businesses must also consider the ethical implications of using AI in customer experience strategies. Transparency in how customer data is collected and used is paramount to building trust. Customers are increasingly wary of data privacy concerns, and businesses that prioritize ethical AI practices will likely gain a competitive edge. By communicating openly about data usage and ensuring robust security measures, SMEs can not only enhance their customer experience but also foster long-term relationships built on trust and respect.

Data-Driven Decision Making

Data-driven decision making is increasingly becoming a cornerstone for SMEs looking to leverage AI effectively. In an era where data is generated at an unprecedented rate, the ability to interpret and utilize this information can set a business apart from its competition. For SMEs, tapping into data analytics allows for more informed choices, reducing the reliance on intuition alone. By integrating AI tools into their operations, these businesses can analyze customer behavior, market trends, and operational efficiency, leading to strategic advancements that were once the reserve of larger corporations.

The first step in adopting a data-driven approach is to establish a clear framework for data collection and analysis. SMEs should focus on identifying key performance indicators (KPIs) that align with their business goals. This could involve tracking customer engagement metrics, sales conversions, or supply chain efficiencies. Once these KPIs are established, businesses can leverage AI-driven analytics platforms to gather insights. These platforms can sift through vast amounts of data to identify patterns and trends, providing actionable insights that can guide decision-making processes. By translating raw data into meaningful information, SMEs can make more proactive and strategic decisions.

Moreover, data-driven decision making empowers businesses to personalize customer experiences. With AI, companies can analyze customer data to understand preferences and behaviors, allowing for tailored marketing strategies and product offerings. This personalization leads to improved customer satisfaction and loyalty, which are crucial for the survival and growth of SMEs. Furthermore, the integration of AI tools in customer relationship management (CRM) systems can streamline interactions and enhance service delivery, reinforcing the importance of a data-centric approach in building strong customer relationships.

However, the journey toward data-driven decision making is not without its challenges. Many SMEs may struggle with data quality, integration, or even the initial costs of adopting advanced AI technologies. It is essential for business owners to invest in training and resources that can help them navigate these challenges. Implementing robust data governance policies will also ensure that data is accurate, secure, and compliant with regulations. By overcoming these hurdles, SMEs can unlock the full potential of their data and drive innovation within their organizations.

In conclusion, data-driven decision making represents a transformative opportunity for SMEs in the age of AI. By embracing this approach, SMEs can enhance their competitiveness, drive customer engagement, and optimize operational efficiencies. As the business landscape continues to evolve, the ability to harness data effectively will not only be a trend but a necessity. For those who embrace it, the future holds immense potential for growth and success, while those who resist may find themselves at a disadvantage in a rapidly changing environment.

CHAPTER 3: FIVE MISCONCEPTIONS

"I mean with artificial intelligence we're summoning the demon."

Elon Musk

Warned at MIT's AeroAstro Centennial Symposium

1. Misconception: AI as a Job Killer

Many fear AI will replace human jobs across various sectors, including manufacturing, customer service, and creative industries. This belief creates anxiety about job displacement, particularly in SMEs that rely heavily on

human labor for routine tasks.

Reality:

While AI can automate repetitive tasks, it doesn't necessarily eliminate jobs—it transforms them. AI can take over mundane, time-consuming activities, allowing employees to focus on more strategic, creative, and value-added work. For example, customer service representatives can transition from answering basic inquiries to engaging with customers on more complex issues, using AI tools as support. Additionally, the growth of AI technologies creates new roles, such as AI trainers, data analysts, and machine learning engineers, which SMEs can tap into. Rather than reducing jobs, AI can lead to job evolution, upskilling opportunities, and the creation of new roles that complement human strengths. Embracing AI in an SME environment can drive productivity and growth, leading to a more engaged and empowered workforce.

2. Misconception: AI is Only for Large Corporations

Many SMEs believe AI is only accessible to large corporations with deep pockets, leaving smaller businesses feeling excluded from the benefits of AI technology.

Reality:

AI is more accessible to SMEs than ever before. With the rise of cloud-based AI services, SMEs can leverage AI solutions on a subscription or pay-per-use basis, often without needing a large upfront investment. These tools cover a range of applications—customer service chatbots, automated marketing, predictive analytics, and more— allowing small businesses to streamline operations, improve customer experiences, and gain competitive advantages. Many AI solutions are designed to be user-friendly and require minimal technical expertise, enabling SMEs to implement them quickly and efficiently. As a result, AI can be a powerful tool for SMEs to level the playing field with larger companies, drive innovation, and compete in the digital marketplace.

3. Misconception: AI Requires Complex, Technical Expertise

Many SMEs assume that adopting AI necessitates a deep technical understanding, including specialized expertise in data science, machine learning, or programming. This can lead to the belief that AI is only suitable for organizations with a dedicated IT department or an in-house team of experts. Business owners may feel overwhelmed by the complexity of AI, assuming they would need to hire specialized talent or invest significant time and resources into understanding and implementing these technologies.

Reality:

While certain advanced AI applications may require specialized knowledge, many AI tools are now designed to be user-friendly and accessible for non-technical users. Numerous cloud-based AI platforms offer pre-built models, automation workflows, and intuitive interfaces, which make it easy for SMEs to implement AI solutions without deep technical expertise. Additionally, many AI tools are plug-and-play, requiring minimal setup and offering comprehensive support. This shift makes AI increasingly accessible to businesses of all sizes, empowering SMEs to leverage the technology without the need for a highly technical workforce.

4. Misconception: AI is Too Expensive for SMEs

Many small business owners believe that AI is out of their budget, imagining it requires significant investment in expensive hardware, software, and infrastructure.

Reality:

The cost of AI has decreased significantly, making it accessible to SMEs at a fraction of the cost it once was.

Many AI tools are available through cloud-based services with affordable subscription pricing, meaning SMEs only pay for what they use, without the need for costly infrastructure. These solutions can lead to significant cost savings by automating routine tasks, reducing human error, and improving operational efficiency. For example, AI-driven tools can optimize inventory management, enhance marketing targeting, and improve customer engagement—all of which can boost profitability. With minimal upfront costs, AI can offer a high return on investment for SMEs that strategically implement it into their operations.

5. Misconception: AI is Too Time-Consuming to Implement

Some SMEs believe that integrating AI into their operations would be an arduous and time-consuming process that could disrupt their existing workflows. The idea of implementing AI might seem overwhelming, especially for small businesses that already have limited resources or personnel. Business owners may worry that AI adoption would involve significant downtime, retraining staff, or even a complete overhaul of their current systems.

Reality:

Implementing AI doesn't necessarily have to be complex or disruptive. Many AI tools are designed for easy integration into existing workflows and systems. For example, AI-powered customer support platforms, like chatbots, can be integrated into a website or social media channels with minimal setup. Similarly, automated marketing tools or data analytics platforms often come with pre-configured templates that can be quickly adapted to a business's needs. SMEs can start small, with pilot projects or incremental integrations, and scale up as they gain confidence in the technology. Moreover, many AI providers offer dedicated support and training, helping businesses navigate the transition smoothly and with minimal impact on daily operations.

CHAPTER 4: KEY AI TRENDS TO WATCH

"Someone on TV has only to say, 'Alexa,' and she lights up. She's always ready for action, the perfect woman, never says, 'Not tonight, dear.'"

Sybil Sage

As quoted in a New York Times article

Machine Learning Advancements

Machine learning has rapidly evolved over the past few years, transforming how businesses operate and interact with customers. For SMEs, understanding these advancements is crucial for leveraging technology to

remain competitive. Machine learning enables systems to learn from data patterns, allowing businesses to automate processes, enhance customer experiences, and make data-driven decisions. As algorithms become more sophisticated, the potential applications for SMEs are expanding, providing opportunities that were previously reserved for larger corporations.

One of the most significant advancements in machine learning is the development of Natural Language Processing (NLP). NLP allows machines to understand and interpret human language, which can be a game-changer for SMEs looking to improve customer service. Chatbots powered by NLP can handle customer inquiries around the clock, providing instant support and freeing up human resources for more complex tasks. Additionally, sentiment analysis tools can help businesses gauge customer feedback from social media or reviews, enabling them to respond proactively to concerns and improve their offerings.

Another notable trend is the rise of Automated Machine Learning (AutoML), which simplifies the process of developing machine learning models. Previously, creating effective models required expertise in data science, which could be a barrier for many small business owners. With AutoML, businesses can leverage user-friendly platforms that guide them through the model-building process, democratizing access to advanced analytics. This advancement allows SMEs to harness the power of data without needing a dedicated team of data scientists, enabling them to compete on a more level playing field.

The integration of machine learning with other technologies, such as the Internet of Things (IoT) and big data analytics, is also reshaping business operations. For example, IoT devices can collect vast amounts of data from various sources, which machine learning algorithms can analyze to identify trends and optimize processes. This synergy can lead to improved inventory management, predictive maintenance, and enhanced supply chain efficiency. SMEs that adopt these integrated solutions can significantly reduce costs and improve operational efficiency, positioning themselves for growth in an increasingly digital marketplace.

Finally, as machine learning continues to advance, ethical considerations and data privacy remain at the forefront of discussions. Business owners must navigate the challenges posed by regulations and public concern over data handling. Adopting transparent practices and prioritizing data protection will not only build trust with customers but also ensure compliance with emerging regulations. By strategically implementing machine learning while adhering to ethical standards, SMEs can harness its power responsibly, turning potential challenges into opportunities for sustainable growth and innovation.

Natural Language Processing Innovations

Natural Language Processing (NLP) has evolved significantly in recent years, transforming the way businesses interact with their customers and manage internal operations. For SMEs, understanding these innovations can be pivotal in leveraging AI effectively. NLP technologies enable machines to understand, interpret, and respond to human language in a valuable way, enhancing customer service, streamlining workflows, and providing insights that were previously hard to obtain. As these innovations continue to develop, they present unique opportunities and challenges for businesses in every industry.

One of the prominent advancements in NLP is the rise of conversational AI, which includes chatbots and virtual assistants. These tools allow companies to provide 24/7 customer support, answering queries and resolving issues without the need for human intervention. For small businesses, implementing a chatbot can be a cost-effective solution to improve customer engagement and satisfaction. Many of these systems are now powered by sophisticated machine learning algorithms that continually learn from interactions, becoming more effective over time. This not only saves time for business owners but also helps in maintaining a consistent customer experience.

Sentiment analysis is another critical innovation in NLP that can significantly benefit SMEs. By analyzing customer feedback, social media posts, and reviews, businesses can gauge public sentiment towards their products and services. This insight allows business owners to make data-driven decisions regarding marketing strategies, product development, and customer engagement practices. By understanding the emotional tone of customer interactions, businesses can tailor their approaches to better meet the needs of their audience, fostering loyalty and improving brand perception.

Moreover, NLP innovations are increasingly being integrated into data analytics tools, providing businesses with enhanced capabilities to analyze and interpret large volumes of unstructured data. SMEs can utilize these tools to identify trends, customer preferences, and market opportunities that might have gone unnoticed in traditional data analysis. This ability to harness data more effectively can lead to improved decision-making and strategic planning, ultimately contributing to a competitive advantage in a crowded marketplace.

As the landscape of NLP continues to evolve, it is essential for SMEs to stay informed about the latest trends and technologies. By embracing these innovations, businesses can not only improve operational efficiency but also enhance customer experiences. However, it is crucial to approach these technologies thoughtfully, considering factors such as data privacy and ethical implications. As AI becomes an integral part of business operations, understanding how to leverage NLP effectively will be key to navigating the future of AI, determining whether it serves as a friend, trend, or potential obstacle for their business.

AI in Cybersecurity

As SMEs increasingly rely on digital platforms for operations and customer engagement, the need for robust cybersecurity measures has never been more critical. Cyber threats are evolving rapidly, and traditional security measures are often inadequate to combat sophisticated attacks. AI has emerged as a powerful ally in the fight against cybercrime. By leveraging AI, businesses can enhance their security protocols, detect unusual behavior, and respond to threats in real-time, ultimately safeguarding their sensitive data and maintaining customer trust.

AI technologies, such as machine learning and Natural Language Processing (NLP), enable systems to analyze vast amounts of data quickly and accurately. This capability allows for the identification of patterns and anomalies that may indicate a security breach. For instance, AI algorithms can monitor network traffic and detect deviations from normal behavior, flagging potential threats before they escalate. This proactive approach not only helps to prevent data breaches but also minimizes the damage should an incident occur, giving SMEs a fighting chance against cybercriminals.

Moreover, the automation of threat detection and response through AI can significantly reduce the burden on IT teams. SMEs often struggle with limited resources and expertise in cybersecurity. By integrating AI-driven solutions, these businesses can automate routine security tasks, freeing up valuable time for their teams to focus on strategic initiatives. This efficiency allows for a more robust security posture without the need for extensive investments in personnel or infrastructure, making AI a practical tool for businesses of all sizes.

However, the adoption of AI in cybersecurity is not without its challenges. Business owners must be aware of the potential risks associated with relying heavily on automated systems. While AI can enhance security measures, it is not infallible. Cybercriminals are also leveraging AI to develop more sophisticated attacks, making it essential for businesses to maintain a balanced approach. This includes combining AI-driven solutions with human oversight and ongoing employee training to ensure that everyone within the organization is aware of the latest threats and best practices for maintaining cybersecurity.

Ultimately, the integration of AI in cybersecurity represents a crucial trend for SMEs. As cyber threats continue to evolve, those who embrace AI technologies will be better positioned to defend against attacks and protect their assets. By understanding the benefits and limitations of AI in cybersecurity, business owners can make informed decisions that will not only enhance their security measures but also contribute to the overall growth and sustainability of their enterprises in an increasingly digital world.

CHAPTER 5: IMPLEMENTING AI IN YOUR BUSINESS

"The development of full artificial intelligence could spell the end of the human race."

Stephen Hawking

Told the BBC

Assessing Your Needs and Goals

Assessing your needs and goals is a crucial first step for SMEs considering the integration of AI into their operations. To effectively harness AI, it's essential to have a clear understanding of what your business requires and

the specific outcomes you want to achieve. Start by evaluating your current processes and identifying areas that could benefit from AI solutions, such as customer service, inventory management, or data analysis. This assessment will help you prioritize which functions to optimize and ensure that the implementation of AI aligns with your overall business strategy.

Next, consider the scalability of your goals. SMEs often operate with limited resources, making it imperative to choose AI applications that can grow alongside your company. Establishing measurable objectives will allow you to track progress and adjust your approach as necessary. For instance, if your goal is to improve customer engagement, you might set targets related to response times or satisfaction ratings. By breaking down larger aspirations into achievable milestones, you can maintain motivation and focus while navigating the complexities of AI integration.

Another key aspect of assessing your needs is understanding the potential challenges associated with AI adoption. This includes not only the financial implications but also the technological infrastructure required to support AI tools. Evaluate your existing systems and determine if they can accommodate new AI technologies. Additionally, consider the skills of your current workforce. Identifying gaps in expertise will help you plan for necessary training or hiring, ensuring your team is prepared to leverage AI effectively.

Moreover, it's essential to consider ethical implications and customer perceptions related to AI usage. Transparency with your customers about how you are using AI can build trust and enhance your brand reputation. Assess how your audience might respond to AI-driven initiatives and ensure that your goals align with their values and expectations. This consumer-centric approach can inform your decisions and foster a stronger relationship with your customer base, which is vital for sustained growth.

Finally, revisit and refine your needs and goals regularly. The landscape of AI is continually evolving, and so are the needs of your business. As you implement AI solutions, gather feedback and data to assess their effectiveness, and be prepared to pivot your strategy as new trends emerge. This ongoing evaluation will not only help you maximize the benefits of AI but also position your business as a forward-thinking entity in an increasingly competitive market. By being proactive in assessing your needs and goals, you can ensure that AI serves as a valuable ally in your business journey.

Choosing the Right AI Tools and Solutions

Choosing the right AI tools and solutions is crucial for SMEs navigating the rapidly evolving landscape of AI. With numerous options available, understanding the specific needs of your business is the first step in making informed decisions. A well-defined strategy will help you identify which tools can enhance productivity, streamline operations, and ultimately contribute to your bottom line. By aligning AI solutions with your business objectives, you can maximize the return on your investment and position your organization for sustainable growth.

One of the key considerations when selecting AI tools is the level of integration with your existing systems. Many businesses rely on a combination of software for various functions, such as customer relationship management, inventory management, and marketing automation. When evaluating AI solutions, look for tools that can seamlessly integrate with your current platforms. This compatibility not only reduces the friction of implementation but also ensures that data can flow freely between systems, leading to more accurate insights and better decision-making.

Cost is another critical factor in the selection process. SMEs often operate with tighter budgets, making it essential to evaluate the pricing structure of AI solutions.

Some tools may require significant upfront investment, while others operate on a subscription model that can be more manageable over time. Additionally, consider the long-term costs associated with maintenance, updates, and potential scaling as your business grows. A clear understanding of the total cost of ownership will help you avoid unexpected expenses and ensure that the chosen solution remains viable as your needs evolve.

User-friendliness and support are also vital when choosing AI tools. Many business owners may not have extensive technical expertise, so it's essential to select solutions that are intuitive and easy to use. Look for platforms that offer comprehensive training resources and customer support to assist your team during the onboarding process. A responsive support team can make a significant difference in addressing issues that arise, allowing you to maintain productivity and focus on your core business activities.

Finally, consider the scalability of the AI solutions you are evaluating. As your business grows, your needs will change, and the tools you choose must be able to adapt accordingly. Opt for solutions that offer flexibility in features and pricing, allowing you to expand functionality as needed. This foresight will ensure that your investment in AI continues to deliver value, helping you stay competitive in a rapidly changing market. By taking these factors into account, SMEs can confidently choose AI tools that will not only support their current operations but also drive future success.

Developing an AI Integration Strategy

Developing an AI integration strategy is essential for SMEs looking to harness the power of AI. This process begins with a clear understanding of the specific needs and objectives of the business. Owners should assess their current operations and identify areas where AI can provide the most benefit, such as improving customer service, streamlining processes, or enhancing data analysis. A tailored approach ensures that the AI initiatives align with the overall business goals, maximizing the potential return on investment.

Once the objectives are established, businesses need to evaluate the available AI technologies that can meet these needs. This involves researching various tools and platforms that offer AI capabilities, such as chatbots for customer interaction, predictive analytics for inventory management, or machine learning algorithms for personalized marketing. It is crucial for business owners to stay informed about the latest advancements in AI, as the landscape is constantly evolving. Engaging with industry experts or attending relevant workshops can provide valuable insights into the most suitable technologies for their specific niche.

After selecting the appropriate technologies, the next step is to develop a comprehensive implementation plan. This should include a timeline for deployment, a budget allocation, and a strategy for training employees on the new systems. Involving team members early in the process can foster a sense of ownership and ease the transition. Additionally, it is essential to establish clear metrics for success to evaluate the effectiveness of the AI integration. Regular assessments will help identify areas for improvement and ensure that the technology continues to meet the changing needs of the business.

Moreover, businesses must consider the ethical implications and data privacy concerns associated with AI integration. Understanding the legal landscape surrounding data usage and ensuring compliance with regulations such as the General Data Protection Regulation (GDPR) is paramount. This not only protects the business from potential legal issues but also builds trust with customers who are becoming increasingly aware of their data rights. Implementing transparent AI practices will enhance the company's reputation and can differentiate it from competitors who may overlook these considerations.

Finally, ongoing evaluation and adaptation of the AI strategy are critical as the business grows and technology advances. AI is not a one-time investment but rather a continuous journey that requires regular updates and refinements. Business owners should remain agile, ready to pivot their strategies based on new information or changing market dynamics. By fostering a culture of innovation and being open to feedback from employees and customers alike, SMEs can effectively leverage AI as a strategic partner, ensuring they remain competitive in an increasingly digital landscape.

CHAPTER 6: THE ETHICAL CONSIDERATIONS OF AI

"AI will be the most transformative technology since electricity."

Eric Schmidt

ex-CEO, Alphabet (Google)

Data Privacy and Security

Data privacy and security are critical considerations for SMEs as they navigate the integration of AI into their operations. With the increasing reliance on data-driven decision-making, understanding how to protect sensitive

information has become paramount. The rise of AI technologies, which often require vast amounts of data for training and implementation, poses unique challenges in ensuring that data privacy is maintained. SMEs must adopt robust security measures to safeguard customer information while remaining compliant with evolving regulations.

The General Data Protection Regulation (GDPR) and the California Consumer Privacy Act (CCPA) are examples of legislative frameworks that emphasize the importance of data privacy. For SMEs utilizing AI, these laws mandate transparency in data usage and give consumers rights over their personal information. Non-compliance can lead to significant penalties, making it essential for business owners to stay informed about their responsibilities. Implementing AI solutions requires a thorough understanding of these regulations to avoid legal repercussions and build trust with customers.

To enhance data security, SMEs should consider adopting a multi-layered approach that incorporates both technology and policy measures. This includes using encryption to protect data in transit and at rest, implementing firewalls, and employing intrusion detection systems. Additionally, regular training for employees on data security best practices can help mitigate risks associated with human error. As AI technologies evolve, so do the tactics used by cybercriminals. Therefore, maintaining a proactive stance on cybersecurity is vital for preventing data breaches that could jeopardize the business's reputation and financial stability.

Moreover, SMEs should evaluate the AI tools they adopt critically. Not all AI solutions are created equal when it comes to data privacy and security. Business owners should conduct thorough due diligence on vendors, ensuring they have robust security protocols and compliance measures in place. Engaging with third-party security experts can also provide valuable insights and strategies for enhancing data protection. By prioritizing the selection of AI tools that align with their security needs, SMEs can leverage technology effectively without compromising sensitive information.

Finally, fostering a culture of data privacy within the organization can significantly impact overall security. SMEs should prioritize open communication about the importance of data protection among employees and encourage reporting of potential vulnerabilities. By integrating data privacy into the company's core values, businesses can create a more secure environment that respects customer information. As AI continues to shape the future of commerce, SMEs that prioritize data privacy and security will not only protect their assets but also position themselves as trustworthy entities in an increasingly digital marketplace.

Bias in AI Algorithms

Bias in AI algorithms is a significant concern for SMEs as they integrate these technologies into their operations. AI systems learn from historical data, which can inadvertently carry biases present in that data. These biases may arise from various factors, including societal prejudices, unrepresentative training datasets, or flawed data collection methods. As businesses increasingly rely on AI for decision-making processes, understanding and addressing these biases becomes crucial to ensure fair and equitable outcomes.

The implications of biased AI algorithms can be profound, particularly in areas such as hiring, customer service, and marketing. For instance, an AI recruitment tool trained on historical hiring data might favor candidates from specific demographics, thereby perpetuating existing inequalities. This not only affects the fairness of hiring practices but can also lead to a lack of diversity within the workforce. For SMEs looking to attract top talent, this could hinder their ability to compete and innovate in an increasingly diverse marketplace.

Moreover, biased AI can lead to misinformed business strategies. When AI tools are used for customer segmentation or targeted marketing, biases in the underlying data can skew results and lead to ineffective campaigns. If an AI model overemphasizes certain customer traits while neglecting others, it can result in missed opportunities and wasted resources. For business owners, ensuring that AI models are trained on comprehensive and representative datasets is essential for achieving accurate insights that drive growth.

To combat bias in AI algorithms, business owners must adopt a proactive approach. This includes implementing regular audits of AI systems to identify and rectify bias, as well as diversifying the datasets used for training. Collaborating with AI vendors who prioritize ethical AI practices can also help mitigate risks. Additionally, fostering an organizational culture that values diversity and inclusion can positively influence the development and deployment of AI technologies, ensuring they align with broader business goals.

Ultimately, addressing bias in AI algorithms is not just a technical challenge but a strategic imperative for SMEs. By recognizing and mitigating these biases, business owners can enhance the effectiveness of their AI applications, promote fairness, and build a stronger reputation in the marketplace. As AI continues to evolve, those who prioritize ethical considerations in their technology adoption will be better positioned to thrive in the future landscape of business.

Building Trust with AI

Building trust with AI is a crucial aspect for SMEs who are navigating the complexities of integrating AI into their operations. Trust is foundational, particularly in a landscape where the reliability and transparency of technology are under scrutiny. Business owners must recognize that fostering trust involves not only the technology itself but also the relationships built with customers, employees, and partners. By understanding the nuances of AI and its implications, businesses can develop a framework that enhances credibility and reliability.

One of the first steps in building trust with AI is ensuring transparency in how AI systems operate. Business owners should strive to communicate clearly about the capabilities and limitations of their AI tools. Providing customers with insights into how decisions are made—such as the data inputs, algorithms used, and the rationale for outputs—can demystify AI processes. This transparency not only alleviates potential fears but also empowers customers to make informed decisions. When businesses openly share how AI influences their services, they establish a foundation of trust that can lead to stronger customer loyalty.

Data privacy and security are paramount concerns for consumers, and addressing these issues is essential for building trust in AI applications. SMEs must adopt robust data protection measures and comply with relevant regulations. It is important to communicate these safeguards to customers, demonstrating a commitment to protecting their information. By prioritizing data security and being proactive in addressing potential vulnerabilities, businesses can reassure customers that their personal information is safe, which in turn fosters a trusting relationship.

Another critical element in establishing trust is the ethical use of AI. Business owners should be aware of the ethical implications associated with AI technologies, including biases in algorithms, the potential for discrimination, and the broader societal impacts of AI deployment. By committing to ethical practices, such as regularly auditing AI systems for fairness and inclusivity, businesses can mitigate risks and enhance their reputation. Engaging with stakeholders to gather feedback on AI practices further illustrates a dedication to ethical standards, reinforcing trust among consumers and the community.

Finally, fostering a culture of continuous improvement and responsiveness can significantly enhance trust in AI initiatives. Business owners should actively seek customer feedback on AI-driven services and be willing to adapt based on that input. By demonstrating a willingness to learn and evolve, businesses can show that they value their customers' experiences and opinions. This responsive approach not only reinforces trust but also positions businesses to stay ahead of trends and challenges in the AI landscape. As SMEs navigate the future of AI, prioritizing trust will be essential for thriving in an increasingly interconnected and technology-driven world.

CHAPTER 7: CASE STUDIES OF AI SUCCESS IN SMES

"AI is not only for engineers. It brings changes in the dynamic of business, and we have to adapt or die."

Satya Nadella

CEO, Microsoft

Retail Industry Innovations

The retail industry has witnessed transformative innovations in recent years, driven largely by advancements in AI. As SMEs seek to navigate this rapidly changing landscape, understanding these

innovations is crucial to staying competitive. From personalized shopping experiences to inventory management, AI is reshaping how retailers operate, enabling them to meet customer demands more efficiently and effectively.

One of the most significant innovations in retail is the use of AI for personalized marketing. Through data analysis and machine learning algorithms, retailers can gather insights about customer preferences and behaviors. This allows businesses to tailor marketing strategies and product recommendations to individual shoppers. By implementing AI-driven personalization, SMEs / retailers can enhance customer engagement, increase conversion rates, and foster loyalty, ultimately driving sales growth.

Another area where AI is making waves is in supply chain and inventory management. Retailers are now able to utilize predictive analytics to anticipate demand for products, which helps in optimizing inventory levels. This not only reduces the risk of overstocking or stockouts but also leads to significant cost savings. By leveraging these AI tools, small and medium businesses can streamline their operations, improve their cash flow, and respond more dynamically to market trends, which is essential in today's fast-paced retail environment.

Customer service is also undergoing a revolution due to AI innovations. Chatbots and virtual assistants powered by AI are becoming commonplace, enabling retailers to provide 24/7 support to customers. These tools can handle a wide range of inquiries, from product information to order tracking, without the need for human intervention. For SMEs, this means that they can offer enhanced customer service at a fraction of the traditional cost, freeing up resources to focus on other critical areas of their operations.

Finally, the integration of AI in the retail sector is paving the way for innovative in-store experiences. Technologies such as Augmented Reality (AR) and Virtual Reality (VR) are being utilized to create immersive shopping environments that engage customers on a deeper level. For instance, AR can allow customers to visualize how furniture would look in their homes before making a purchase. As these technologies continue to evolve, SMEs / retailers must consider how they can incorporate them to enhance the customer journey and differentiate themselves from competitors. Embracing these innovations will be key to thriving in the future of retail.

AI in Service-Based Businesses

AI is rapidly transforming the landscape of service-based businesses, offering opportunities for efficiency, personalization, and improved customer engagement. For SMEs, understanding how to leverage AI tools can be crucial in staying competitive. From automating administrative tasks to enhancing customer interactions, AI can significantly reduce operational costs and increase productivity. Businesses that adopt AI solutions can streamline workflows, allowing employees to focus on more strategic tasks that require human insight.

One of the most compelling applications of AI in service-based industries is in customer service. Chatbots and virtual assistants are increasingly utilized to handle routine inquiries, providing instant support to customers at any time of the day. This not only improves response times but also enhances customer satisfaction, as clients receive timely answers to their questions. Additionally, AI can analyze customer interactions to identify common issues and trends, enabling businesses to proactively address concerns and tailor their services accordingly.

AI-driven analytics tools also play a pivotal role in understanding customer behavior and preferences. By harnessing data from various touchpoints, businesses can gain insights into what drives customer engagement and loyalty. These tools can segment audiences, allowing for targeted marketing strategies that resonate with specific demographics. For SMEs, such insights can lead to more effective campaigns and improved conversion rates, as resources can be allocated to initiatives that yield the highest returns.

Moreover, AI can enhance operational efficiency by automating repetitive tasks. In service-based businesses, this includes scheduling, invoicing, and even project management. Tools powered by AI can optimize these processes, reducing the likelihood of human error and freeing up valuable time for employees. This operational streamlining not only improves productivity but also allows businesses to scale more easily, as they can handle increased demand without a proportional increase in resources.

However, the integration of AI in service-based businesses does come with challenges. Business owners must navigate concerns regarding data privacy, potential job displacement, and the need for ongoing training and adaptation. As AI technology continues to evolve, staying informed about best practices and ethical considerations will be essential. Embracing AI as a strategic partner rather than a replacement can help SMEs innovate and thrive in an increasingly competitive marketplace.

Manufacturing and AI Optimization

Manufacturing has long been the backbone of many SMEs, providing essential goods and services to consumers. However, the advent of AI has begun to redefine this landscape. By integrating AI technologies

into manufacturing processes, SMEs can enhance efficiency, reduce costs, and improve product quality. AI algorithms can analyze vast amounts of data to optimize production schedules, manage inventory, and predict equipment failures before they occur. This proactive approach allows businesses to minimize downtime and ensure a smoother operation, ultimately leading to increased profitability.

One of the most compelling applications of AI in manufacturing is predictive maintenance. Traditional maintenance schedules often lead to either over-maintenance, which can waste resources, or under-maintenance, resulting in costly breakdowns. AI systems can leverage machine learning to analyze data from machines in real-time, identifying patterns that indicate potential failures. By predicting when a machine is likely to fail, businesses can schedule maintenance at the most opportune times, thereby reducing unexpected shutdowns and extending the lifespan of their equipment. This not only saves money but also enhances productivity.

AI optimization extends beyond maintenance; it also plays a crucial role in supply chain management. SMEs often struggle with inventory management, balancing the need to have enough stock on hand to meet customer demand while avoiding the costs associated with excess inventory. AI tools can analyze sales data, market trends, and seasonal fluctuations to forecast demand more accurately. This enables businesses to optimize their inventory levels, reducing waste and ensuring that they can meet customer needs promptly. By streamlining the supply chain through AI, SMEs can enhance their competitiveness in an increasingly crowded market.

Moreover, AI can support quality control processes in manufacturing. Traditional quality control often relies on manual inspections, which can be time-consuming and prone to human error. AI-driven image recognition systems can quickly and accurately assess product quality during the manufacturing process. These systems can detect defects that might be missed by the human eye, ensuring that only products that meet stringent quality standards reach the market. This not only enhances customer satisfaction but also helps to build a strong reputation for reliability and quality among consumers.

In conclusion, the integration of AI into manufacturing processes presents significant opportunities for SMEs. By optimizing operations through predictive maintenance, efficient supply chain management, and enhanced quality control, SMEs can position themselves for success in a rapidly evolving market. Embracing AI is not just about keeping up with trends; it is about leveraging technology as a strategic ally to drive growth and sustainability. As business owners consider the role of AI in their operations, it is crucial to view it as a friend that can unlock new potential rather than a looming threat to their traditional practices.

CHAPTER 8: CHALLENGES OF ADOPTING AI

"AI is so intelligent it's open to the bad players, the ones that want to trick you about who they are."

Steve Wozniak

co-founder Apple

Understanding Costs and ROI

Understanding the costs associated with implementing AI is crucial for SMEs. AI technologies can vary significantly in price depending on their complexity, the size of the implementation, and the specific needs of the

business. Initial costs may include software licenses, hardware upgrades, and potential consulting fees for integration. Additionally, ongoing maintenance and training for employees are factors that can affect the overall budget. Business owners must take a comprehensive view of all these potential expenses to accurately assess the financial commitment required for AI implementation.

Return on Investment (ROI) is a key metric that businesses use to evaluate the financial benefits of adopting AI. For SMEs, the calculation of ROI can be particularly challenging due to often limited resources and the need for measurable outcomes. ROI should not only consider direct financial gains but also include factors such as enhanced productivity, improved customer satisfaction, and faster decision-making. A thorough analysis can help business owners determine whether the investment in AI will yield substantial long-term benefits.

In addition to calculating direct costs and potential ROI, business owners should examine the broader implications of AI adoption. The integration of AI can lead to transformative changes in operations, often resulting in cost savings that go beyond initial expenses. For example, AI can streamline processes, reduce manual errors, and enable better resource allocation. These efficiencies can contribute to a more agile business model, allowing small and medium enterprises to compete more effectively in their respective markets.

Moreover, understanding the competitive landscape is essential when evaluating the costs and ROI of AI. As more businesses begin to adopt AI technologies, those that hesitate may risk falling behind. Staying ahead of the curve can lead to increased market share and customer loyalty. Therefore, business owners must consider not just the immediate financial implications but also the strategic advantages that come with timely AI investment. This awareness can inform their decisions and help them weigh the long-term benefits against the upfront costs.

Finally, transitioning to an AI-driven approach requires a cultural shift within the organization. Business owners need to foster an environment that embraces innovation and is open to change. This cultural alignment is vital for maximizing the ROI of AI initiatives. Training employees, encouraging collaboration between departments, and maintaining clear communication can enhance the effectiveness of AI tools. By understanding both the costs and the potential ROI, SMEs can make informed decisions that position their companies for future growth and success in an increasingly AI-centric world.

Navigating Technical Barriers

Navigating technical barriers is a crucial aspect for SMEs looking to leverage AI effectively. One of the primary challenges faced by these businesses is the complexity of AI technologies. Many owners may feel overwhelmed by the technical jargon and the rapid pace of advancements in AI. To make informed decisions, it is essential to develop a foundational understanding of AI concepts. Business owners should invest time in educating themselves about the various types of AI applications relevant to their industries, such as machine learning, NLP, and robotics. This knowledge can empower them to identify the right tools and platforms that align with their operational needs.

Another significant barrier is the cost associated with implementing AI solutions. While the long-term benefits of AI can be substantial, the initial investment can be daunting for smaller enterprises. Business owners should explore various funding options, including grants, partnerships with technology providers, and phased implementation strategies. By breaking down the costs into manageable segments and focusing on high-impact areas, businesses can gradually incorporate AI into their operations without jeopardizing their financial stability. Additionally, cloud-based AI solutions often offer more affordable alternatives, enabling businesses to access advanced technologies without the burden of heavy infrastructure costs.

Data privacy and security concerns also present a technical barrier for many businesses considering AI adoption. With AI systems relying heavily on data for training and operation, ensuring the protection of sensitive information is paramount. Business owners need to familiarize themselves with relevant regulations, such as GDPR or CCPA, and implement robust data governance practices. Establishing clear protocols for data collection, storage, and usage can mitigate risks and foster trust among customers. Furthermore, collaborating with cybersecurity experts can provide valuable insights into best practices for protecting data while leveraging AI technologies.

Integration with existing systems poses another challenge when navigating technical barriers. Many SMEs have legacy systems that may not be compatible with new AI solutions. This can lead to operational inefficiencies and increased costs. To address this issue, business owners should conduct a thorough assessment of their current technology landscape and identify areas where AI can enhance operations. Collaborating with IT professionals or consultants can help facilitate smoother integration processes. Moreover, focusing on scalable AI solutions that can evolve alongside the business will allow for a more seamless transition and long-term adaptability.

Finally, the skills gap within the workforce can hinder the successful implementation of AI technologies. Many SMEs may lack personnel with the necessary expertise to manage AI projects effectively. To overcome this barrier, investing in training and development for existing employees is crucial. Business owners should consider offering workshops, online courses, or partnerships with educational institutions to build a more knowledgeable workforce. Additionally, fostering a culture of continuous learning and innovation will encourage employees to embrace AI as a valuable tool rather than a threat. By addressing these technical barriers head-on, SMEs can position themselves to harness the full potential of AI, ensuring they remain competitive in an increasingly technology-driven marketplace.

Workforce Training and Development

Workforce training and development are critical components for SMEs navigating the evolving landscape of AI. As AI technologies advance, the skills required in the workforce are also changing. Business owners must recognize the importance of equipping their employees with the necessary tools and knowledge to leverage AI effectively. This proactive approach not only enhances productivity but also fosters a culture of innovation within the organization, ensuring that the workforce is prepared to meet the demands of a rapidly changing market.

Investing in training programs that focus on AI-related skills will empower employees to understand and utilize these technologies. This includes training in data analysis, machine learning principles, and the ethical implications of AI. By providing tailored training sessions, workshops, and online courses, SMEs can create a workforce that is not only competent in using AI tools but also capable of identifying opportunities for integration within their specific business processes. This investment in human capital is essential for maintaining a competitive edge in an increasingly automated world.

Moreover, fostering a mindset of continuous learning is vital for businesses looking to thrive in the era of AI. As technology continues to evolve, so too will the skills needed to harness its potential. Encouraging employees to engage in ongoing education and professional development will ensure that they remain adaptable and resilient. This can be achieved through mentorship programs, partnerships with educational institutions, and participation in industry conferences. By cultivating a culture that values learning, SMEs can create a dynamic workforce that is better equipped to navigate the challenges posed by AI advancements.

Collaboration between businesses and technology providers is another important aspect of workforce training and development. By working closely with AI vendors, SMEs can gain insights into the latest tools and applications available in the market. These partnerships can facilitate customized training programs that align with specific business needs, helping employees to gain hands-on experience with AI systems. In turn, this collaboration can lead to innovative applications of AI that drive efficiency and enhance customer experiences, ultimately contributing to the growth and sustainability of the business.

In conclusion, workforce training and development are essential for SMEs seeking to harness the potential of AI as a friend rather than a foe. By investing in skill development, fostering a culture of continuous learning, and collaborating with technology providers, business owners can ensure that their teams are well-prepared to adapt to the challenges and opportunities presented by AI. Embracing this proactive approach will not only enhance operational efficiency but also position SMEs as leaders in their respective industries, ready to thrive in the future of AI.

CHAPTER 9: THE FUTURE LANDSCAPE OF AI

"We are confident in our ability to build AGI and are shifting our focus to superintelligence."

Sam Altman

CEO, OpenAI

Predictions for AI Development

As AI continues to evolve, SMEs must stay informed about the potential trajectories of AI development. Predictions surrounding AI's future often emphasize its role as a transformative force across various industries.

Many experts suggest that AI will increasingly become integrated into everyday business operations, enhancing efficiency and productivity. For companies that adapt early, this presents an opportunity to streamline processes, reduce costs, and improve customer experiences. However, businesses that fail to recognize the importance of adapting to these advancements may find themselves at a competitive disadvantage.

One significant trend in AI development is the growing emphasis on accessibility. Cloud-based AI solutions are becoming more affordable and user-friendly, allowing SMEs to leverage advanced technologies without the need for extensive resources or expertise. This democratization of AI tools means that even companies with limited budgets can implement AI-driven analytics, customer service chatbots, and marketing automation systems. As these tools become more widespread, businesses that utilize them effectively are likely to outperform those that do not.

Another prediction is the increased focus on ethical AI. As consumers become more aware of data privacy and the ethical implications of AI technologies, businesses will need to prioritize transparency and responsible AI practices. This shift will not only enhance customer trust but also create a competitive edge for companies that commit to ethical standards. SMEs that proactively address these concerns by ensuring compliance with regulations and adopting ethical guidelines will likely attract a more loyal customer base.

The integration of AI with other emerging technologies, such as the Internet of Things (IoT) and blockchain, is also anticipated to reshape the business landscape. This convergence will enable companies to harness vast amounts of data in real-time, fostering smarter decision-making processes. For SMEs, this means not only optimizing operations but also creating new revenue streams and business models. Those that can effectively integrate these technologies will position themselves for growth in an increasingly interconnected world.

Finally, the ongoing development of AI will likely lead to a shift in workforce dynamics. While some fear job displacement due to automation, many experts believe that AI will complement human workers rather than replace them. SMEs can benefit from this by focusing on reskilling employees to work alongside AI systems. By fostering a culture of continuous learning and adaptation, businesses can enhance their workforce's capabilities, ensuring they remain competitive in an evolving market. Embracing AI as a collaborative partner rather than a threat will be crucial for long-term success.

The Role of AI in Business Evolution

The integration of AI into business operations has become a pivotal factor in the evolution of SMEs. AI technologies are reshaping how businesses function, offering tools that streamline processes, enhance decision-making, and improve customer engagement. For SMEs which often face resource constraints, AI presents an opportunity to level the playing field against larger competitors. By automating routine tasks and providing data-driven insights, AI allows these businesses to focus on strategic initiatives that drive growth.

One of the most significant roles AI plays in business evolution is through data analytics. SMEs often struggle with the sheer volume of data generated from their operations and customer interactions. AI algorithms can analyze this data at unprecedented speeds, uncovering trends and patterns that human analysts might miss. This capability enables SMEs to make informed decisions based on real-time insights, whether it's optimizing inventory, improving marketing strategies, or enhancing customer service. As businesses leverage AI-driven analytics, they can respond more effectively to market changes and customer needs.

Moreover, AI is transforming customer interactions through personalized experiences. Chatbots and virtual assistants are increasingly being adopted by SMEs to provide 24/7 customer support, answer inquiries, and facilitate transactions. This not only improves customer satisfaction but also allows businesses to allocate human resources to more complex tasks. By utilizing AI in customer engagement, businesses can create a tailored experience that fosters loyalty and encourages repeat business. The ability to provide immediate and relevant responses to customer needs is a key differentiator in today's competitive landscape.

In addition to enhancing operations and customer relations, AI can also drive innovation within SMEs. With AI tools, businesses can experiment with new ideas, products, and services with reduced risk. For instance, machine learning models can predict market trends, enabling businesses to pivot or expand their offerings based on anticipated demand. Furthermore, AI can streamline the product development process by analyzing customer feedback and preferences, ensuring that new products resonate with target audiences. This innovative capacity is essential for SMEs aiming to differentiate themselves and stay ahead in a rapidly evolving market.

81

However, the adoption of AI is not without challenges. SMEs must navigate issues such as technology integration, data privacy, and the potential for job displacement. Understanding the implications of AI on workforce dynamics is crucial, as the technology may alter traditional roles and require new skill sets. Business owners must also ensure that their use of AI aligns with ethical standards and regulations to maintain customer

trust. By addressing these challenges proactively, SMEs can harness the transformative power of AI while mitigating potential risks, ensuring that their evolution is both sustainable and responsible.

Preparing for an AI-Driven Market

The emergence of AI has significantly transformed the marketplace, compelling SMEs to adapt their strategies to remain competitive. Preparing for an AI-driven market involves understanding how AI technologies can enhance business operations, customer engagement, and decision-making processes. Businesses must first educate themselves about the various applications of AI, from customer service chatbots to data analytics tools that can provide insights into consumer behavior. By familiarizing themselves with these technologies, business owners can identify which AI solutions align with their objectives and foster growth.

In addition to understanding AI tools, it is crucial for business owners to assess their current technological infrastructure. Many SMEs may initially lack the necessary systems to effectively implement AI solutions. Evaluating existing processes and technologies can highlight areas where upgrades or new installations are needed. Investing in robust IT infrastructure not only facilitates the integration of AI but also ensures data security and compliance with regulations, which are vital in an increasingly digital landscape.

Training employees to work alongside AI is another essential step in preparing for this transition. As AI systems take on more routine tasks, employees can focus on higher-level responsibilities that require human insight and creativity. Business owners should consider investing in training programs that help staff understand AI technologies, their benefits, and how to use them effectively. This investment not only enhances employee skill sets but also fosters a culture of innovation within the organization, making it more agile in responding to market demands.

Moreover, SMEs must develop a strategy for data management and utilization. AI thrives on data, and the quality of insights derived from AI systems is directly linked to the data fed into them. Implementing practices that ensure accurate data collection, storage, and analysis is essential. Business owners should consider leveraging customer relationship management (CRM) systems and data analytics platforms to consolidate data effectively. By doing so, they can harness AI capabilities to better understand customer preferences and improve product offerings.

Finally, ethical considerations surrounding AI adoption should not be overlooked. As businesses integrate AI into their operations, they need to be aware of the potential implications on privacy and employment. Establishing clear policies that prioritize ethical AI use can build trust with customers and employees alike. This proactive approach not only mitigates risks associated with AI implementation but also positions a business as a responsible player in the market, potentially enhancing its reputation and customer loyalty in an AI-driven economy.

CHAPTER 10: EMBRACING AI FOR BUSINESS GROWTH

"The risk of extinction from AI should be a global priority."

Geoffrey Hinton

Considered the Godfather of AI

Summary of Key Takeaways

The rapid evolution of AI presents both opportunities and challenges for SMEs. One of the key takeaways is the importance of understanding AI as a tool rather than a replacement. AI can enhance operational efficiency, improve customer engagement, and provide valuable

insights through data analysis. By leveraging AI technologies, business owners can streamline processes, reduce costs, and ultimately increase profitability.

Another significant takeaway is the necessity of adopting a proactive approach to AI integration. Businesses that wait to implement AI strategies may find themselves at a competitive disadvantage. Early adopters can capitalize on the advantages of AI, such as automation and predictive analytics, which can lead to improved decision-making and strategic planning. This foresight not only prepares businesses for future market demands but also positions them as leaders in their respective industries.

Furthermore, understanding the ethical implications of AI is crucial for maintaining customer trust and loyalty. As AI systems become more prevalent, consumers are increasingly concerned about data privacy and the ethical use of AI technologies. Business owners must prioritize transparency in their AI practices and ensure compliance with regulations. By fostering a culture of ethical AI use, companies can mitigate risks and reinforce their brand reputation in the eyes of consumers.

Collaboration with technology partners is another vital aspect highlighted. SMEs may lack the resources to develop AI solutions in-house, making it essential to seek partnerships with tech firms that specialize in AI. This collaboration can facilitate access to advanced technologies and expertise that might otherwise be out of reach. By forming strategic alliances, businesses can enhance their AI capabilities, ensuring they remain competitive in an increasingly digital landscape.

Finally, continuous education and adaptation are imperative in the fast-paced world of AI. Business owners should commit to ongoing learning about AI trends and technologies to stay informed and agile. Embracing a mindset of innovation and flexibility will enable them to pivot as necessary and harness the full potential of AI. By doing so, SMEs can not only thrive amid technological advancements but also set the stage for sustained growth and success in the future.

Actionable Steps for SMEs

To harness the potential of AI, SMEs must take actionable steps that align with their unique business needs. The first step for SMEs is to assess their current operations and identify areas where AI can add value. This involves evaluating processes such as customer service, inventory management, marketing, and sales. By pinpointing specific pain points or inefficiencies, business owners can determine where AI solutions can provide the most significant benefits, whether through automation, improved data analysis, or enhanced customer engagement.

Once potential areas for AI implementation are identified, SMEs should prioritize these opportunities based on their potential ROI. Business owners can create a roadmap that outlines short-term and long-term goals, focusing on projects that will deliver the quickest wins first. This strategic approach allows SMEs to allocate resources effectively, ensuring that initial AI investments yield measurable results. Additionally, by demonstrating quick wins, businesses can build momentum and gain stakeholder buy-in for more extensive AI initiatives in the future.

Education and training are crucial for the successful integration of AI technologies. SMEs should invest in upskilling their workforce to ensure that employees are equipped to work alongside AI tools. This could involve hosting workshops, providing online courses, or partnering with educational institutions to create tailored training programs. By fostering a culture of continuous learning, businesses can mitigate fear and resistance to change, empowering employees to embrace AI as a tool that augments their capabilities rather than replaces them.

Collaboration with technology partners is another essential step for SMEs looking to implement AI solutions. Many AI technologies are complex and may require expertise that small business owners do not possess in-house. By seeking partnerships with tech firms or consultants specializing in AI, SMEs can access the knowledge and resources needed to successfully deploy AI initiatives. These collaborations can also provide insights into best practices and emerging trends, ensuring that businesses stay ahead of the curve in a rapidly changing technological landscape.

Finally, SMEs must prioritize data management and security as they adopt AI technologies. Effective AI systems rely on high-quality data, so businesses should establish robust data collection and analysis processes. Additionally, as they handle more customer and operational data, SMEs need to implement strong cybersecurity measures to protect sensitive information. Regular audits and compliance checks can help businesses maintain data integrity and build trust with customers, ensuring that the benefits of AI implementation are realized without compromising security.

The Road Ahead: Staying Ahead of the Curve

The landscape of AI is evolving rapidly, presenting both opportunities and challenges for SMEs. As AI technologies become more sophisticated, understanding their implications is crucial for staying competitive. The road ahead is marked by an increasing reliance on AI tools and solutions, which can streamline operations, enhance customer experiences, and drive innovation. Embracing this technology is not just a trend; it is essential for survival in a market that is becoming increasingly automated and data-driven.

To navigate this landscape, business owners must first understand the various forms of AI and their applications. From machine learning algorithms that predict consumer behavior to chatbots that enhance customer service, the potential uses of AI are vast. By investing time in learning about these technologies, owners can identify which solutions align best with their business needs. This knowledge empowers them to make informed decisions about integrating AI into their operations, ensuring they harness its capabilities effectively.

Collaboration with AI experts and technology partners is another critical step in staying ahead of the curve. Many SMEs may lack the resources to develop AI solutions in-house. By partnering with technology providers, they can gain access to cutting-edge tools and expertise without the hefty investment typically associated with custom development. Such collaborations can also offer insights into industry best practices, enabling businesses to implement AI in ways that enhance their competitive edge and operational efficiency.

Moreover, cultivating a culture of innovation within the organization is essential for leveraging AI effectively. Business owners should encourage their teams to explore new ideas and experiment with AI applications. Training employees to understand and utilize AI tools can foster a more agile workforce capable of adapting to changes brought on by technological advancements. This proactive approach not only prepares the organization for future challenges but also positions it as a leader in its industry.

Finally, staying informed about regulatory developments and ethical considerations surrounding AI is vital. As the technology evolves, so too do the guidelines governing its use. Business owners must remain vigilant about compliance with emerging regulations to avoid potential pitfalls. Additionally, addressing ethical concerns, such as data privacy and algorithmic bias, can enhance a company's reputation and build trust with customers. By prioritizing these aspects, SMEs can navigate the road ahead with confidence, ensuring that they not only survive but thrive in the age of AI.

CHAPTER 11: THE CURRENT LANDSCAPE AND THE FUTURE OF AI

"Artificial intelligence and generative AI may be the most important technology of any lifetime."

Marc Benioff

Chair, CEO, and co-founder, Salesforce

As we enter 2025, AI has undergone remarkable advancements, transforming various industries. It has transcended mere buzzword status, fundamentally altering how businesses operate, innovate, and engage with their customers. The breakthroughs in AI we see today are paving the way for even more revolutionary

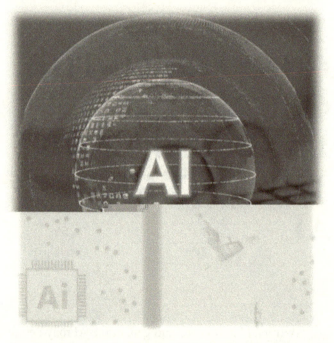

developments in the future. This book delved into the present state of AI, its potential for the future, and offers insights on how businesses can harness these developments to succeed.

The AI Landscape in 2025

The present landscape of AI is characterized by remarkable advancements, with numerous types of AI actively addressing real-world challenges. These include:

Narrow AI (Weak AI): This is the predominant type of AI in use today, specialized in performing specific functions such as image recognition, language comprehension, data analysis, and product recommendations. Common examples of narrow AI that we encounter daily include virtual assistants like Siri, chatbots, and tailored shopping suggestions.

General AI (AGI - Strong AI): Although it remains mostly a theoretical concept, AGI signifies a significant advancement in AI. This form of AI would possess the capability to think, learn, and adapt across various tasks, effectively imitating human cognitive processes. Currently, we do not have genuine AGI, but experts anticipate its potential emergence within the next 1 to 3 years.

Superintelligence: This concept refers to a potential

future in which AI exceeds human intelligence across nearly all domains. While there is a wide range of predictions regarding the timeline for achieving superintelligence, some experts speculate it could become a reality in the next 5 years. Nonetheless, it remains a speculative idea, with numerous challenges to overcome before reaching this stage.

The Future of AI: What to Expect

As we move forward, AI is set to expand and develop further, with a significant potential to influence the business landscape. Here are several ways AI will impact the future:

Enhanced Forecasting: With ongoing advancements in AI, companies will gain the ability to anticipate trends and understand consumer behavior with remarkable precision. This will lead to better-informed decisions and more impactful strategies.

Automating Complex Processes: Although AI has made strides in automating straightforward tasks, its future will involve managing more intricate operations. In industries such as healthcare, finance, and manufacturing, AI will enhance workflows that once relied heavily on human skills, leading to greater efficiency and precision.

Partnership Between Humans and AI: Looking ahead, AI will complement rather than replace human capabilities. It will analyze vast datasets, generate insights, and propose alternatives, while humans will contribute creativity, intuition, and strategic vision to propel innovation forward.

Enhancements in Communication: Advances in Natural Language Processing (NLP) will keep evolving, leading to smoother customer service interactions and enabling businesses to connect with their customers in ever more personalized manners.

Supporting Small Businesses: SMEs will gain access to the same AI resources utilized by larger companies, enabling them to assess market trends, improve customer service, and streamline operations—all at a significantly lower cost.

Ethical Considerations: As AI increasingly integrates

into business processes, organizations must prioritize the development of ethical guidelines to guarantee transparency and accountability in decisions made by AI systems.

The Role of AI in Accelerating Business Growth

The future of business is intricately linked to AI. It's not merely about staying competitive; it's about leveraging AI to discover new opportunities and lead the industry. Here are ways in which AI will propel growth in the coming years:

Enhanced Decision-Making: AI will facilitate more informed business decisions by examining vast quantities of data and generating insights that would be challenging, if not unachievable, for humans to discover independently. Whether it's regarding a merger, the launch of a new product, or market expansion, AI will empower organizations to base their decisions on data rather than intuition.

Advanced Virtual Assistants: In the future, virtual

assistants are expected to significantly enhance their capabilities. They will assist with a wide range of tasks, from organizing schedules to preparing reports, becoming essential resources for business leaders. As their intelligence grows, these assistants will also offer recommendations for optimizing processes and strategies informed by data insights.

Where Creativity Integrates with AI: AI will serve as a valuable partner in the creative process. From designing new logos and crafting compelling marketing campaigns to generating innovative product ideas, AI will tackle much of the demanding work, allowing businesses to enhance their innovation speed and efficiency.

Advanced Customer Service: AI-driven customer support systems will advance to become intelligent, empathetic agents proficient in resolving intricate issues. By understanding context and emotions, these systems will provide incredibly personalized experiences, ensuring that customers feel recognized and appreciated.

Sustainability and Efficiency: AI is set to be instrumental in enhancing the sustainability of businesses.

By minimizing energy usage and streamlining waste management, AI will assist companies in making their operations more environmentally friendly and economically efficient—an objective that is becoming increasingly vital for both businesses and consumers.

The Effects of AI on Employment and the Workforce

Given the numerous advantages that AI offers to businesses, the effects on the job market cannot be overlooked. Numerous positions are likely to be automated, resulting in substantial changes across various industries. Below are some key areas where AI is anticipated to make a major difference:

Customer Service Positions: With the advancement of AI chatbots and virtual assistants, a significant number of customer service roles may be phased out. These technologies will take care of standard inquiries and tasks, while human agents will continue to be essential for addressing more complicated issues.

Data Entry Positions: Automation through AI is

transforming data entry roles by streamlining manual data processing. This technology excels at performing repetitive tasks with greater speed and precision than humans, leading to a decline in the availability of traditional data entry jobs.

Manufacturing Jobs: The growth of robotics and AI-powered automation in manufacturing is expected to accelerate. A significant number of tasks that are presently handled by human workers on production lines will likely be automated, especially in sectors such as automotive manufacturing and electronics assembly. By 2030, the need for human workers in this field may decrease considerably.

Retail Positions: The rise of AI technologies, including automated checkout systems, inventory management tools, and delivery robots, is set to transform many conventional retail jobs. As a result, retail employees will need to transition into new roles that prioritize customer experience and strategic thinking over manual tasks.

Although these transformations might result in some job displacement, it's essential to recognize that AI will also generate new opportunities. The demand for AI specialists, data scientists, and positions focused on AI governance and ethics is expected to grow. Additionally, roles emphasizing creativity, strategy, and interpersonal skills are likely to become more significant as AI takes over more repetitive tasks.

By 2030, numerous entry-level positions in areas such as customer service and data entry are expected to be automated. However, this shift will pave the way for the creation of new industries and roles, allowing employees to engage in more strategic and creative contributions.

CONCLUSION: THE IMPACT OF AI ON BUSINESS DEVELOPMENT

"AI is one of the most profound things we're working on as humanity. It's more profound than fire or electricity."

Sundar Pichai

CEO of Google and Alphabet

AI has evolved beyond a mere tool for large corporations; it has become a vital element for businesses of all sizes. By optimizing operations and improving customer interactions, AI empowers companies to grow and innovate in previously unthinkable ways. However, the

secret to thriving in this new landscape lies not just in embracing AI, but in strategically leveraging its potential to discover new growth avenues and instigate significant transformation.

As AI advances, businesses that adopt it will be more

equipped to succeed in a rapidly digital and competitive landscape. By leveraging AI thoughtfully and innovatively, organizations can not only navigate disruptions but also take the lead in driving them. The future is driven by AI, and those who embrace these changes will define the business landscape ahead.

ABOUT THE AUTHOR:

"Advances in AI are making it possible to do more with less, and that's going to improve the quality of life for billions of people."

Mark Zuckerberg

CEO of Meta Platforms (Facebook)

Robert Culpepper has a BSc in Engineering and has been an entrepreneur for 20+ years with experience in computer software, design, and technology. He has also held roles in sales, marketing, operations, and senior management; working with startups, SMEs, large corporations / government contractors (including HP and Lockheed-Martin), and the US government. He possesses a unique blend of practical knowledge and strategic insight into driving revenue and business growth.

Robert serves as a fractional Chief Marketing Officer (fCMO) and Chief Growth Officer (fCGO), helping businesses craft effective growth strategies and navigate the complexities of AI adoption. His approach blends innovation with practicality, empowering businesses to leverage AI for tangible success.

This book shares his insights on AI and its transformative impact on small and medium enterprises (SMEs), making it an invaluable resource for business owners and decision-makers looking to embrace the future of AI.

Robert continues to explore the intersection of business strategy and emerging technologies, staying at the forefront of the rapidly evolving AI landscape.

Robert can be found at **RobertCulpepper.me**